SCHIRMER'S LIBRARY
OF MUSICAL CLASSICS

Vol. 2024

LOUIS MOREAU GOTTSCHALK

Collected Works

For Piano

ISBN 978-0-7935-5096-8

G. SCHIRMER, Inc.

DISTRIBUTED BY

HAL•LEONARD®
CORPORATION
7777 W. BLUEMOUND RD. P.O. BOX 13819 MILWAUKEE, WI 53213

CONTENTS

BAMBOULA
Danse de Nègres

Revised and fingered by
Arthur Hochman

Louis Moreau Gottschalk

Op. 2

4

avec expression, mais bien rythmé
con espress., ma ben ritmato
Il canto ben marcato

marcato il basso

To Her Majesty Donna Maria, Queen of Portugal

LA SAVANE
(The Savannah)
Ballade Créole

Op. 3

* May be played by both hands if desired.

LE BANANIER
Chanson nègre

Revised and fingered by
Arthur Hochman

Op. 5

Une corde, sans presser
una corda, senza stringere

28

LE MANCENILLIER
(West Indian Serenade)

Edited and fingered by
R. de Roode

Op. 11

To Richard Hoffman

THE BANJO

Fantasie grotesque

Op. 15

44

48

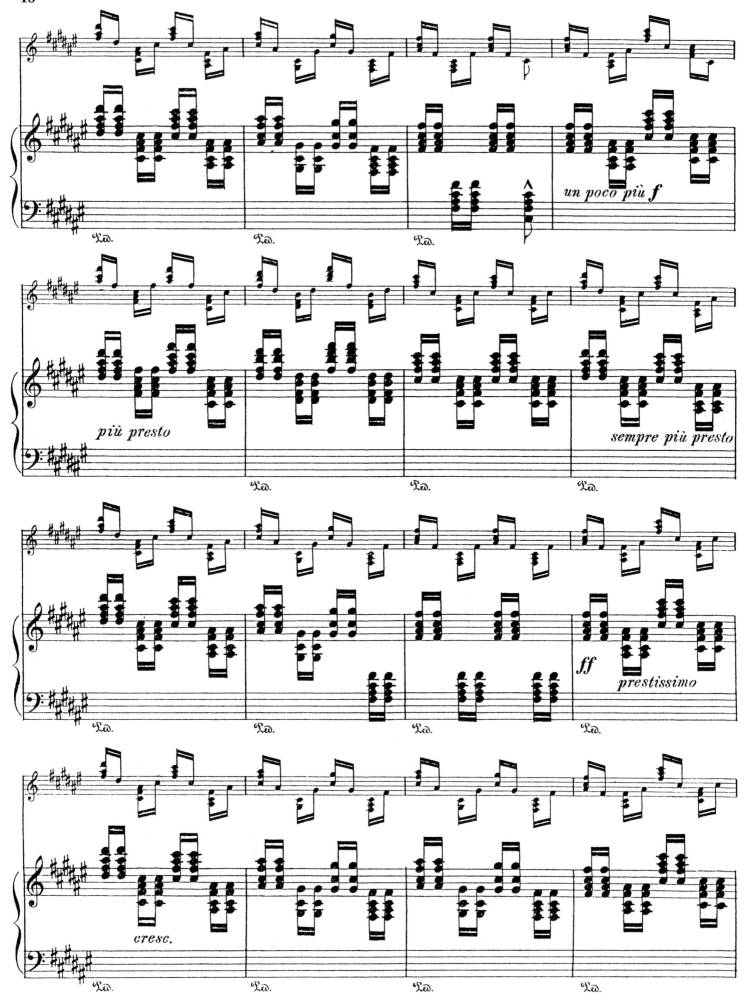

THE LAST HOPE
Meditation

Edited and fingered by
Louis Oesterle

Op. 16

Religioso

*) easier:

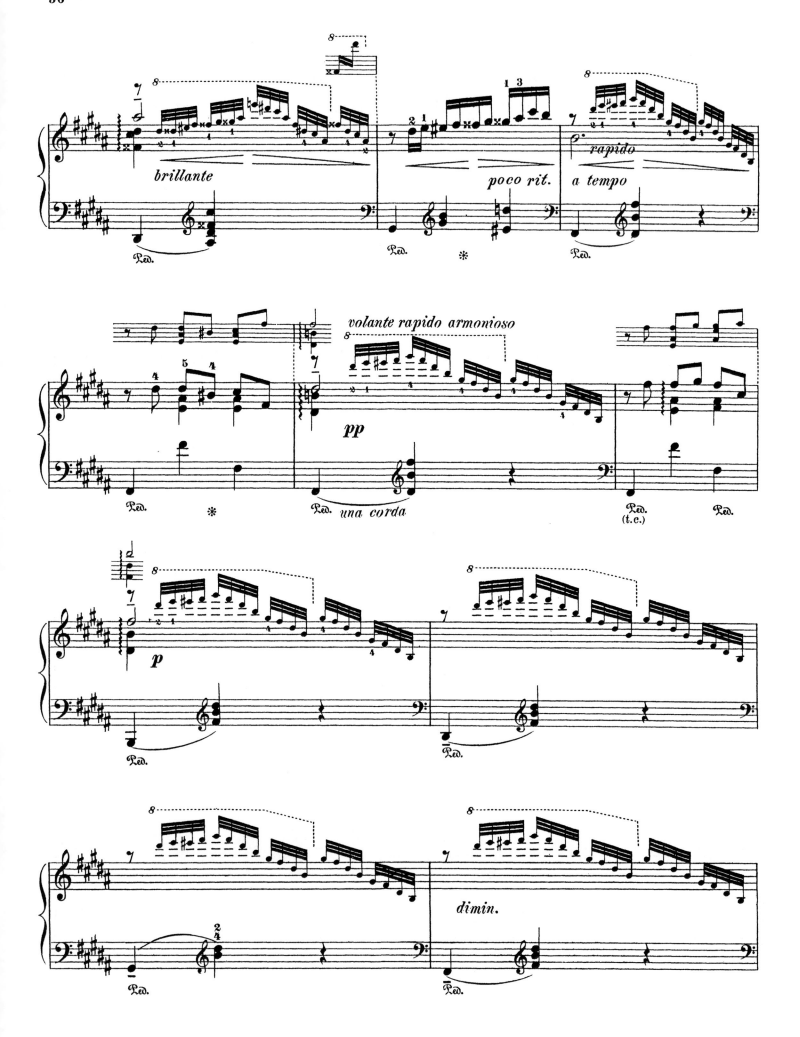

MARCHE DE NUIT

Edited and fingered by
Louis Oesterle

Op. 17

Tempo di Marcia
Moderato

LA SCINTILLA
(The Spark)
Mazurka sentimentale

Edited and fingered by
Louis Oesterle

Introduzione
Moderato

Op. 21

VALSE POÉTIQUE

Sospiro

Edited and fingered by
Louis Oesterle

Op. 24

As played by the composer

RICORDATI

Nessun maggior dolore,
Che ricordarsi del tempo felice
Nella miseria.
Dante: Divina comedia

Edited and fingered by
Louis Oesterle

Op. 26

SOUVENIR DE PORTO RICO

Moderato, ma con moto

92

To my old friend Edouard Verger of St. Pierre, Martinique

DANZA

Op. 33

Moderato quasi andantino

con amore

con abbandono

rapido

8va

pp

una corda

1) Early editions have:

OJOS CRIOLLOS
(Les Yeux créoles)
Danse cubaine

Edited and fingered by
Louis Oesterle

Op. 37

á Mademoiselle Maria Luisa del Rio Noguerido y de Sedano de la Havane

SOUVENIR DE LA HAVANE
Grand Caprice de Concert

*Arranged for piano
by Wachtmann*

Op. 39

Tempo I

PRINTEMPS D'AMOUR MAZURKA

Caprice de concert

Edited and fingered by
Louis Oesterle

Op. 40

BERCEUSE
Cradle-Song

Edited and fingered by
Louis Oesterle

Op. 47

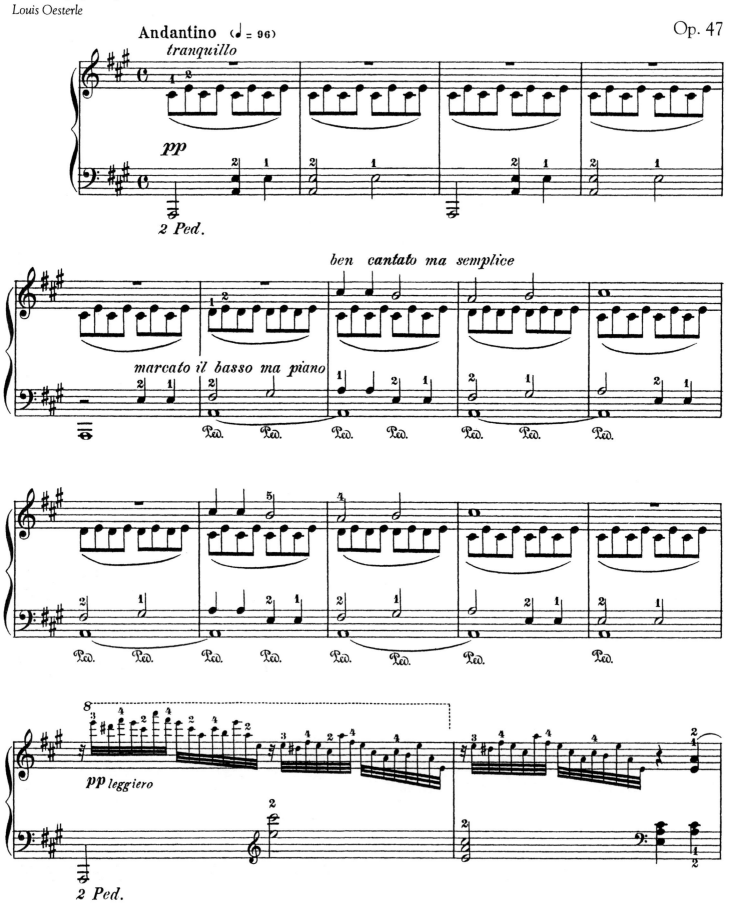

á Monsieur le Général G. B. McClellan

L'UNION
(Paraphrase de Concert Sur les Airs Nationaux)

Op. 48

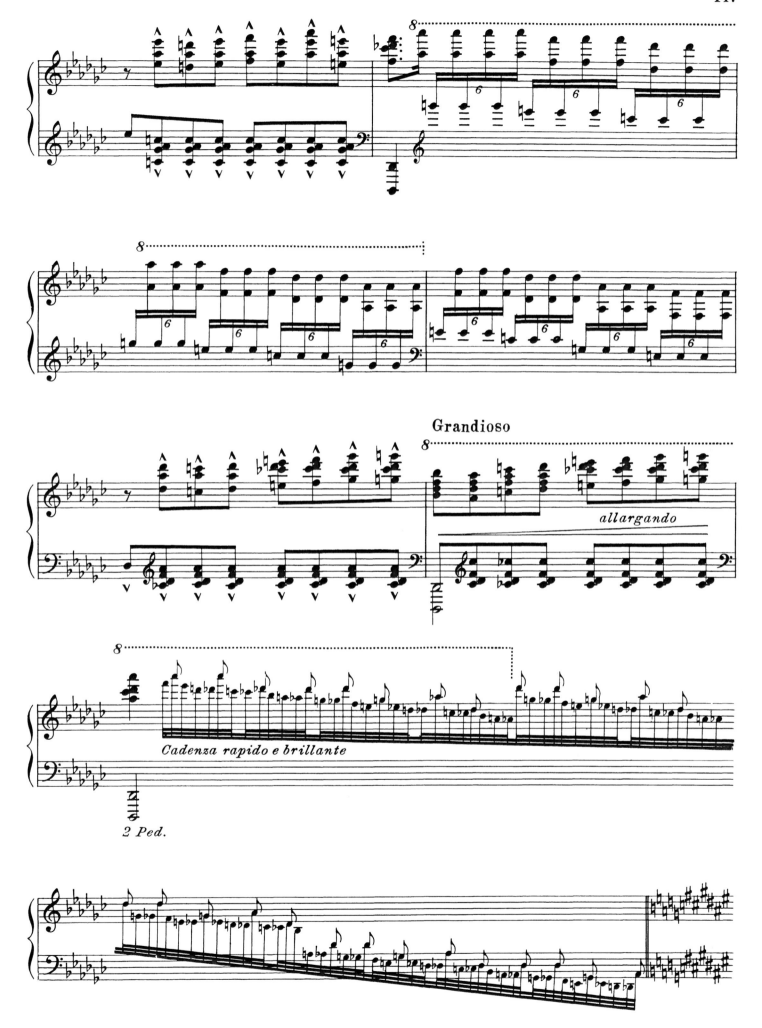

The Star Spangled Banner

1) Possibly :

1) Some editions have:

2) See note, previous page.

Tempo I

con bravura

[♩ = 132]
stridente

❋ Trombe

L.H. R.H.

f
vibrante

(*f*)

❋ Like a trumpet fanfare.

(Hail, Columbia)

Yankee Doodle

Hail Columbia

á mon ami F. G. Hill, de Boston

LA COLUMBE
(The Dove)
Petite Polka

Edited and fingered by
Louis Oesterle

Op. 49

ben marcato il basso

á Madame Mary Eugénie Martin (née Curlett)
de Baltimore

HOME SWEET HOME

Edited and fingered by
Louis Oesterle

Op. 51

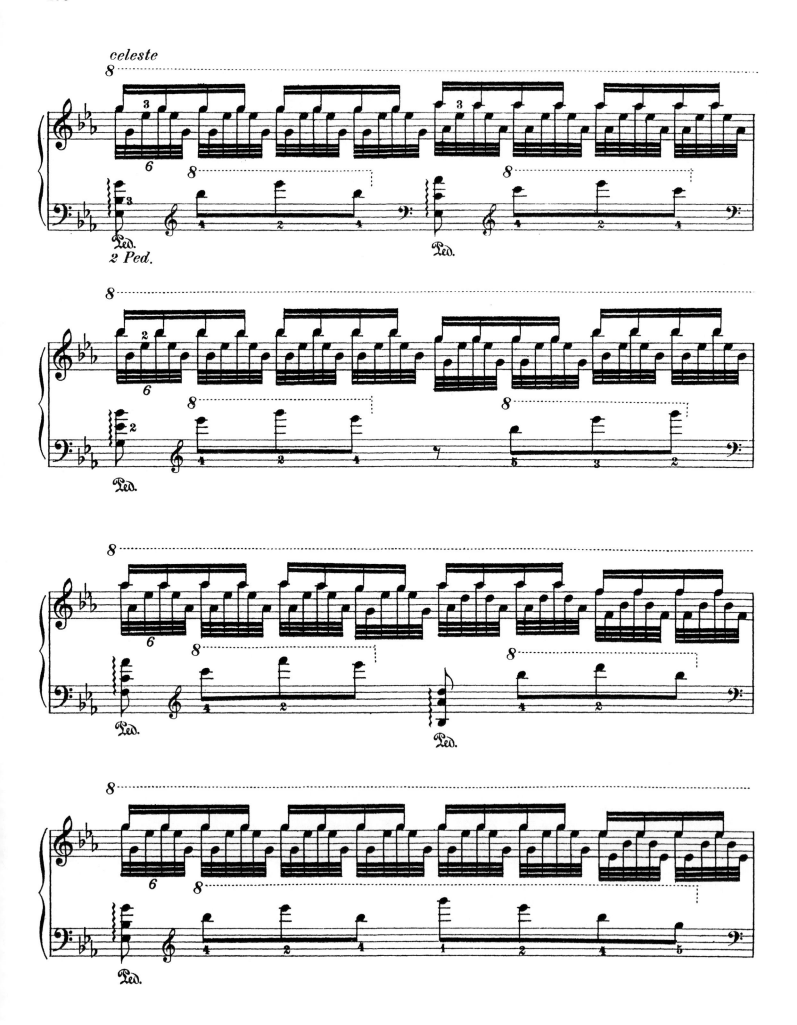

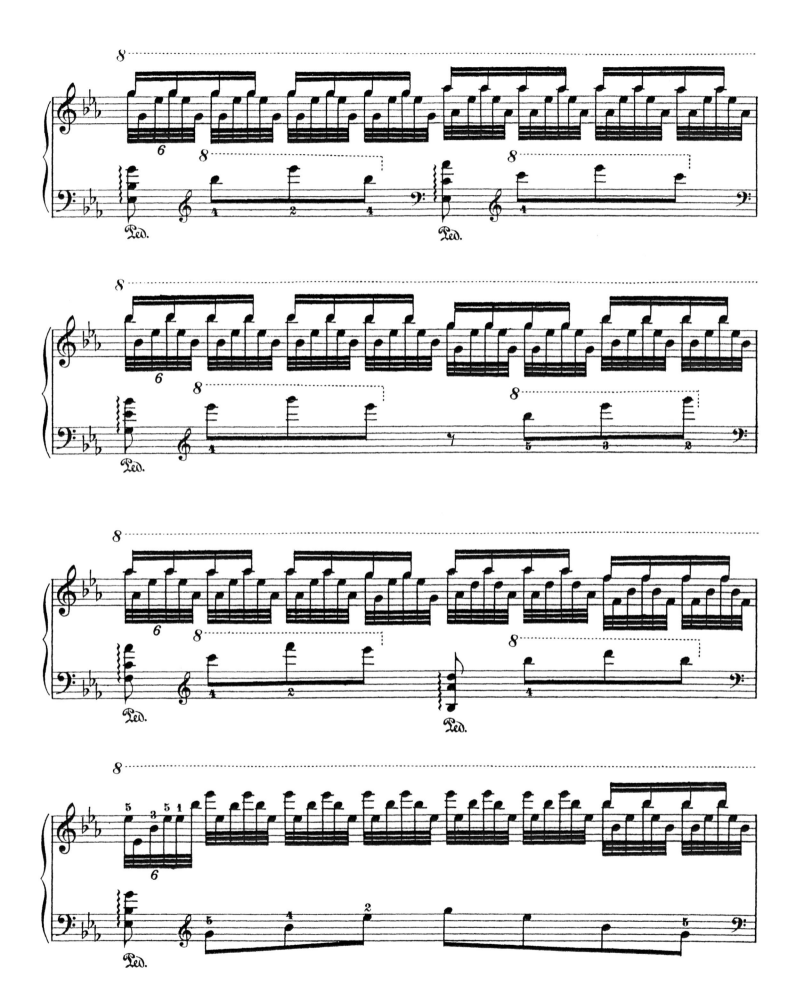

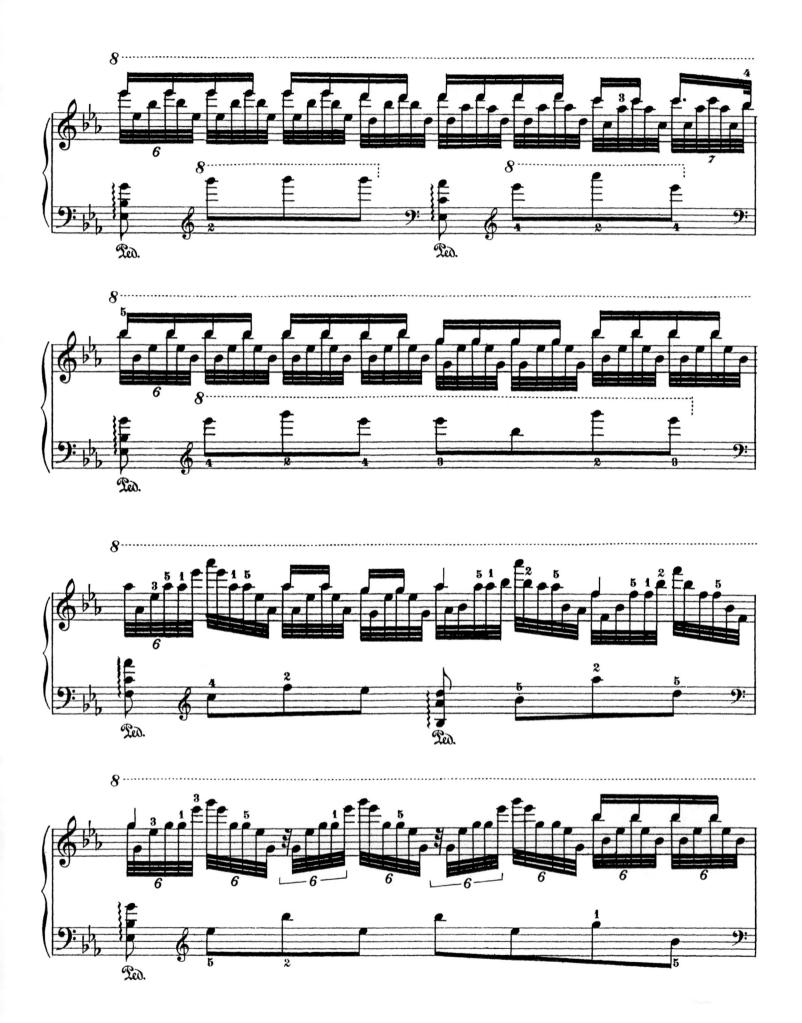

marcato il canto

LA GALLINA
(The Hen)
Cuban Dance

Op. 53

Allegro moderato

á Madame G. Henriques

LE POÈTE MOURANT
(The Dying Poet)
Méditation

Edited and fingered by
Louis Oesterle

1864

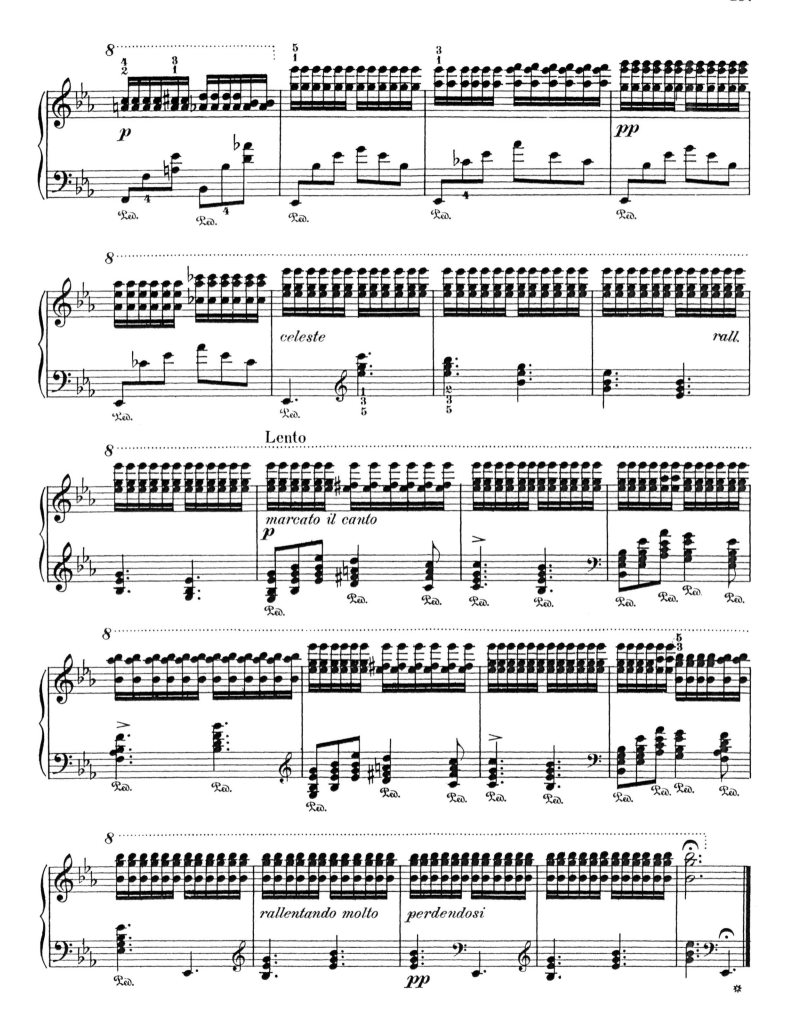

PASQUINADE
(Caprice)

Op. 59